Praise for
14 MUST-HAVE SKILLS FOR MANAGING YOUR STRESS

"This book touched me as a psychiatrist because it makes people aware of the damage caused by stress and of the solutions provided to avoid it. I highly recommend this interesting book, which allows people exposed to stress to find small, effective ways to escape its harmful consequences. There are many stressors on a daily basis, a real burden, and this book will show you how to protect yourself from them."

—**Hana Hajj-Chahine,** psychiatrist and professor at Saint-Joseph University, Lebanon

"A must-read book for people in modern societies who struggle with stress. This book turns into a useful, practical guide to help the reader deal with stress through building skills and attitudes toward life. The practical examples and metaphors help the reader to better understand the meaning of the book."

—**Vicky Marouli,** Msc, CBT psychotherapist and mindfulness instructor

"Backed by a solid amount of research, real-life examples, and an excellent writing style, this book gives the reader an insight into what stress is and how to better manage it in the workplace and at home. The book is short, practical, and enjoyable. I highly recommend this book to whomever is looking to take back control of their life's journey."

—**Mr. Sarkis Naoum,** prominent analyst and columnist in the widely circulated Lebanese newspaper, *An-Nahar*, and author of several publications

14 Must-Have Skills For Managing Your Stress

DON'T LIVE YOUR LIFE WITHOUT THEM

HANI SPIRO FAKHOURI

VIRGINIA BEACH
CAPE CHARLES

14 Must-Have Skills for Managing Your Stress
by Hani Spiro Fakhouri

© Hani Spiro Fakhouri

ISBN 979-8-88824-111-0

All rights reserved. No part of this publication may be reproduced,
stored in a retrieval system, or transmitted in any form or by any means—
electronic, mechanical, photocopy, recording, or any other—
except for brief quotations in printed reviews,
without the prior written permission of the author.

Published by

3705 Shore Drive
Virginia Beach, VA 23455

800-435-4811

TABLE OF CONTENTS

—◁o▷—

Why I Wrote This Book | 11

Introduction | 13

Skill #1: Compartmentalize Your Life | 18

Skill #2: Consider the Worst-Case Scenario | 25

Skill #3: How to Make an Important Decision | 29

Skill #4: Occupy Yourself Constantly | 36

Skill #5: Don't Mind the Futilities | 39

Skill #6: Use Probabilities to Control Your Stress | 42

Skill #7: Accept What You Cannot Avoid or Change | 45

Skill #8: Count Your Blessings | 48

Skill #9: Keep a Positive Mental Attitude | 51

Skill #10: Never Quit | 55

Skill #11: How to Deal With Criticism | 60

Skill #12: Relax | 63

Skill# 13: Dealing With Stress in the Workplace | 66

Skill #14: Exercise Consistently | 72

Conclusion | 77

This book is dedicated to my late father,
Doctor Spiro Fakhouri,
my mother, Zeina Fakhouri,
my sister, Hala Fakhouri,
my wife, Roula,
and my two beautiful daughters,
Maria and Dalia.

WHY I WROTE THIS BOOK

◀◦▶

Living in today's world can be extremely stressful. Our lives are way more complex than those of our parents and grandparents. The need to be constantly connected (via social media, emails, internet, etc.), trying to do too much at the same time (working, parenting, studying, socializing, competing, etc.), living up to other people's expectations or society's norms, being continuously exposed to air, noise, and visual pollution, etc. can all quickly add up and culminate in stress. In 2021, Gallup, a global analytics and advisory firm, asked adults in 122 countries and areas if they went through five different negative experiences on the day before the survey. The results: 42 percent of adults worldwide said they experienced a lot of worry, 41 percent experienced a lot of stress, 28 percent experienced sadness, and 23 percent experienced anger. What a calamity!

Stress affects everyone irrespective of their gender, age, religion, and social status. Unfortunately, no human being is immune to it. Left uncontrolled and unmanaged, chronic or severe stress can have disastrous effects on the body and mind: headaches, heartburn, increased depression, low sex drive, insomnia, weakened immune system, high blood sugar, risk of heart attack, and that is just to name a few! The potential harm that stress causes not only impacts the stressed person but also his/her normal relationship with his/her surroundings, including friends, family members, significant others, and work colleagues.

I have personally struggled with stress for many years as did many of my friends and family members. I can assure you from my personal experience that struggling with chronic or severe stress is very difficult and unpleasant. In order to better deal with and manage stress, I spent countless hours educating myself about the causes of stress, its symptoms, its short and long-term effects on the body and mind, and the different methods for managing it. Along the years, I came to realize that managing stress is more of a skill than anything else. And like any other skill, it is first learned and then perfected through perseverance and consistent practice. Knowing how to manage stress in today's world is a must-have skill. It is so important that it should be taught in schools and universities as part of their compulsory, basic curriculums.

Considering how important and vital managing stress is, I decided to write a short, simple, and quick-to-read book about the fourteen specific skills that I personally found to be most valuable and effective in managing stress. I hope that you find them useful in your own battle against stress, a battle that you can surely win with a bit of patience and perseverance. Keep this book close to you and refer to it as often as you need until these skills become second nature to you. If you find value in this book, recommend it to those whom you know are struggling with stress and complement the knowledge contained in this book with your own experiences.

> Stress is the trash of modern life—
> we all generate it, but if you don't dispose of it
> properly, it will pile up and overtake your life."
> —Danzae Pace

INTRODUCTION

Stress can energize, and stress can kill. Experiencing a bit of stress is a normal phenomenon of life and even a desirable one, but too much of it can wreak havoc on your body and mind. Never allow stress to take control of your existence.

But what exactly is stress? Stress is the physiological and psychological response of your body that is triggered by a stressor. A stressor is:

1. a new or unexpected life event or situation,

2. which *you perceive* to be challenging or threatening,

3. and over which *you feel* you have little control.

Two keywords that stand out from the above definition are: *perception* and *feeling*. The extent to which you perceive an event to be challenging or threatening and whether you feel you have control over it or not will determine the type and extent of your body's physiological and psychological response to such a stressor. Given the highly subjective nature of perceptions and feelings, different individuals will respond differently to the same exact stressors.

The body, in a natural attempt to cope with a stressor, produces certain stress-related hormones typically known as adrenaline, noradrenaline and glucocorticoids. The function of these hormones is to place the body in a "fight or flight" survival mode. This mode is characterized by several chemical reactions taking place in the body with the aim of getting it ready to fight the stressor or run away from it. Some of the normal physiological manifestations of these chemical reactions are:

- sweating
- tensed muscles
- harder and faster heartbeats
- increased blood pressure
- dilated blood vessels
- increased blood sugar and energy levels
- harder and faster breaths
- more acute senses (sight, hearing, etc.)

As you may have noticed, these physiological manifestations solely aim to supply your body with the necessary short-term strength and energy that it requires to fight the stressor or run away from it.

The more you perceive an event to be challenging or threatening and the less you feel you have control over it, the greater the manifestation of the above physiological symptoms in your body. These symptoms on their own are usually harmless when they are short-lived as they represent the normal defense mechanism of the body against a given stressor.

Stressors can emanate from all sorts of different events and circumstances that you may encounter throughout your existence. Depending on the way *you perceive* and *interpret* them, these could be the following:

- Getting a job promotion
- Changing homes
- Taking an exam
- Going through a divorce
- Getting into a fight with a neighbor or a work colleague
- Getting married
- Losing money
- Failing an exam
- Competing in a marathon
- Losing a job
- Losing a loved one
- Gaining fame

The list is, indeed, endless.

As you may already know, not all stress is bad. A bit of stress energizes the body and mind and readies them for the challenges or threats to come. This is especially true when getting prepared to deliver a speech in public, take an exam, have a job interview, play a competitive sport, deal with a threatening situation, etc. However, it is the long-term exposure of an individual to a stressor and the continued activation of the body's natural defense mechanism to such a stressor that ultimately ends up causing long-term damaging effects on the mind and body.

Long-Term Damaging Effects on the Mind

You may experience the following feelings:

- Anxiousness
- Depression
- Frustration
- Irritation
- Sadness
- Helplessness
- Indecisiveness

Long-Term Damaging Effects on the Body

You may experience the following effects:

- Chronic aches and pains
- Headaches and dizziness
- Increased probability of having a heart attack or a stroke
- General fatigue and trouble sleeping
- High blood pressure
- Digestive problems such as constipation or diarrhea
- Weak immune system
- Acid reflux
- And many others

Managing stress is not an impossible task. It is not a natural gift that only a handful of people are born with. Managing stress is a skill that is learned and practiced just like any other skills that you acquire throughout your life. This book discusses fourteen specific skills that aim to provide you with a winning edge in your fight against stress as long as you commit to practicing them diligently and consistently. This set of skills is meant to help you better manage stress at its source so that the remaining physiological and psychological chain reactions in your body become much more manageable. But why fourteen skills, you may be asking, and not just one or two effective, all-encompassing ones? Because certain skills are more effective than others depending on the concerned individual and the nature of the stressor that he/she is dealing with. So, learn and practice all fourteen skills and then decide for yourself which ones are a better fit for you and under which circumstances.

The sooner you learn to manage your stress, the sooner you will become a healthier, happier, and more fulfilled person. You will find yourself in a much better position to eat healthier, avoid bad habits, exercise more often, sleep better, feel more confident, etc. The benefits are truly immense as much as they are endless, and they are certainly worth your time and efforts.

Each chapter of this book discusses a specific skill for managing your stress. I highly recommend that you pause at the end of each chapter and think about how you could have incorporated such a skill during a previously encountered stressful situation, and certainly make sure to practice it at the first future opportunity.

> "We can easily manage if we will only
> take, each day, the burden appointed to it.
> But the load will be too heavy for us if we carry
> yesterday's burdenover again today, and then add
> the burden of tomorrow before
> we are required to bear it."
> —John Newton

SKILL #1

Compartmentalize Your Life

In my opinion, being able to compartmentalize your life represents the most important skill you need to master to gain better control of your life. Gaining better control of your life will help you manage and reduce your everyday stress and tension. Compartmentalization allows you to determine which of your personal and professional tasks and responsibilities are worthy of your time and effort and then to place these in hermetically separate mental buckets to deal with each one of them more efficiently and productively. This approach applies to all your daily tasks and activities, such as working, exercising, going out, playing with your children, and even sleeping.

What Is Compartmentalization?

Compartmentalization simply means the ability to do the following:

- shut the doors that lead to your past and future,
- decide on the tasks that need to be tackled today according to their importance and urgency,
- place these tasks in a sequence of hermetically separate mental buckets with specific time limits, and
- focus all your energy and efforts on accomplishing each task without allowing any distractions to get past your buckets' hermetic barriers.

Shut the Doors That Lead to Your Past and Future

Compartmentalization begins by shutting the doors that lead to your past and future and throwing away the keys. Your past does not exist anymore, and your future does not exist yet. There is no point in thinking or worrying about either of them. That would only be a complete waste of your time and energy.

The past is only as useful as the lessons learned from your mistakes to forge a better future for yourself. Spending an eternity dwelling on the past won't change a single event in it. Regretting missed opportunities or obsessing about what could or should have been are tantamount to crying over spilled milk. Can you ever scoop spilled milk back into its bottle? Obviously not. So, leave the past where it belongs, in the past, and confidently move forward.

As for the future, it is shaped and defined by how well you live today. A well-lived day gives hope and shapes a better tomorrow. It is perfectly acceptable to think about tomorrow as a way of planning ahead, but there is no sense in living today in fear of tomorrow. Tomorrow depends on so many factors that it is utterly useless to even think about controlling or predicting it.

What really matters is today and today alone. Your past should be no more than a distant dream, and your future should be no more than a vision of hope waiting to be shaped by what you do today and how well you do it.

The above wisdom is not new. It has been evidenced in the Bible, which dates back hundreds of years:

- *"Therefore, do not worry about tomorrow, for tomorrow will worry about itself. Each day has enough trouble of its own"*
  (Matthew 6:34, NIV), and . . .

- *"Give your entire attention to what God is doing right now, and don't get worked up about what may or may not happen tomorrow. God will help you deal with whatever hard things come up when the time comes"*
  (Matthew 6:34, The Message).

Along the same line is a famous quote by Gautama Buddha (a religious teacher who lived in South Asia during the sixth or fifth century and who founded Buddhism) that reads, "The secret of health for both mind and body is not to mourn for the past, nor to worry about the future, but to live the present moment wisely and earnestly."

Decide on the Tasks That Need to Be Accomplished Today

Start each morning by taking a few minutes to plan for the day ahead. You can obviously do this the night before as well. Go through all the tasks that you believe you need to accomplish during the day—whatever comes to your mind. Next, place each of these tasks into one of the below four quadrants, which are based on Eisenhower's Urgent/Important Matrix, to distinguish between what is important and what is merely a distraction. This concept was first developed by Dwight Eisenhower to help him prioritize the many issues that he faced as a US Army general, then as Supreme Allied Commander of NATO Forces, and eventually as the thirty-fourth president of the United States of America.

The most important quadrant where you want to be spending most of your time is *quadrant 2: important but not urgent*. This quadrant includes all the tasks that will steadily get you closer to your personal and professional goals. This quadrant affords you the necessary time to tackle these important tasks in the most productive and efficient manner without the stress and anxiety that accompany the urgent nature of the tasks that belong to *quadrant 1: important and urgent*. However, if not properly attended to, these tasks will ultimately become urgent and start moving from quadrant 2 to quadrant 1. Tasks in quadrant 1 are important tasks that tend to be stressful in nature mainly due to their deadlines and strict consequences if not completed

	Urgent	Not Urgent
Important	Quadrant 1 **DO THEM** Tasks with clear deadlines and strict consequences if not completed on time. Reduce the time you spend here by forseeing and planning for these tasks so that they do't end up in this quadrant in the first place.	Quadrant 2 **SCHEDULE THEM** Tasks without deadlines that get you closer to your personal and professional goarls. Mainly involve strategic thinking and taking initiatives. Spend most of your time here. If unatteneded to, these may become urgent and get relocated to Quadrant 1-do not let that happen.
Not Important	Quadrant 3 **DELEGATE THEM** Tasks which need to be completed but do not require your personal attention. Empower others to complete them on your behalf. Spend as little time as possible here.	Quadrant 4 **DELETE THEM** Tasks which are mainly a distraction and do not get you any closer to your personal and professional goals. Do not spend any time here.

on time. But by properly foreseeing and planning for these important tasks, you will be able to largely keep them at bay in quadrant 2.

Tasks in *quadrant 3: urgent but not important* do not require your personal intervention and can be easily delegated to other people. Therefore, take the necessary time to properly train others to complete these tasks on your behalf and free more of your time for your quadrant 2 tasks. Tasks in *quadrant 4: not important and not urgent* are merely a distraction and should be discarded in their entirety.

Hermetically Separate Your Tasks

Now that you know which tasks you need to work on, place these tasks in a sequence of hermetically separate mental buckets where each bucket includes only one task. Then allocate a specific time limit to each mental bucket during which the relevant task should be completed. Use your best judgement to allocate just about the optimal time needed for its completion. For maximum efficiency and productivity, be sure to schedule all the quadrant 2 tasks (important but not urgent) during the hours of the day when you are most productive and active. Here are a few additional pointers in that regard:

- Each bucket should include only one task. Avoid multitasking and focus only on one task until it is completed or until its relevant time duration expires, whichever is earlier.
- Break up large or complex tasks into smaller, manageable ones and compartmentalize them. Tackling large or complex tasks at once is often debilitating and creates stress and tension.

- Avoid being in more than one mental bucket at the same time. Every mental bucket has its own dedicated time and space and will be duly attended to in due course.

- Make more sense of each task by associating it with a personal or professional goal. This will increase your enthusiasm and focus and will provide you with a sense of achievement as you see your goals slowly materializing.

Focus on accomplishing each task without allowing any distractions.

Once you start working on a task, think of nothing else. Focus on being here and now. Channel all your efforts toward completing the task at hand. At times, certain distractions will get past the hermetic barriers of your mental buckets. Here are some examples:

- your mobile phone keeps ringing,

- you hear a distracting or upsetting comment from a work colleague,

- irrelevant thoughts to the task at hand continuously pop in your head,

- an unforeseen request comes your way, or

- boredom and fatigue set in.

From personal experience, deliberately trying to fight off such distractions mostly ends up reinforcing them. This is because the more you think about them, the stronger their hold is on you. In such cases, some sort of an early conclusion or resolution is needed to put such distractions aside. Instead of fighting off these distractions head-on, consider one or more of the following:

- Take a few seconds to decide whether the distraction merits an interruption. For instance, if a request comes your way, immediately decide whether this is something more important than what you are doing right now or if it can wait until your current task is completed. Once you have made your choice, move past the distraction by steadfastly implementing your decision.

- Recognize the distraction by writing it on paper or a computer and promise to deal with it later. This sort of instant resolution will appease your mind and allow you to put the distraction behind you, knowing that you will deal with it at a more opportune time.

- Completely absorb yourself in your current task. The logic here is that the human brain cannot process two different ideas or thoughts at the exact same time. By patiently focusing all your thoughts on your current task, your brain will automatically weaken all other distractions.

As a final thought, don't forget to allocate a daily mental bucket for your own personal needs, such as listening to music, meditating, reading, volunteering, stretching, etc. Consider this bucket as your reward for a day well lived.

SKILL #1
Compartmentalize your life.

> "Whenever I take a position, I like to imagine what it would be like under the worst-case scenario. In doing so, I minimize the confusion if that situation actually develops. In my view, losses are a very important part of trading. When a loss happens, I believe in embracing it."
> —Gil Blake

SKILL #2

Consider the Worst-Case Scenario

Stress consumes a lot of mental resources. When we are stressed, our brain cannot think clearly. This is commonly referred to as brain fog. Brain fog, a symptom of stress, may lead you to the following:

- procrastinating,
- taking additional time to complete a task,
- feeling more tired and distracted than usual, and having trouble organizing thoughts and reactions.

You may recall those moments where your mind was "jumping" all over the place due to intense feelings of stress that kept intruding on your normal thought processes. Dealing with brain fog necessitates dealing with its underlying cause, namely stress.

What Is the Worst Thing That Can Happen?

One effective three-step approach for your consideration when dealing with stress is as follows:

- Step 1: Take a step back and analyze in detail the situation that you are facing and determine in all honesty what is the worst thing that can happen.

- Step 2: Once you have determined the worst-case scenario, take some time to mentally accept it should it ultimately materialize.

- Step 3: From this moment on, dedicate your time and efforts to finding solutions that allow you to mitigate, as much as possible, the negative consequences of the worst-case scenario, bearing in mind that you have already accepted them should you be unable to mitigate them.

Coming to terms with the worst-case scenario will almost always appease your mind and allow you to channel all your mental resources toward finding appropriate solutions.

An example will make this concept clearer. Suppose that after taking a very important university admission exam, you have the uncomfortable feeling that you will fail it. Your mind starts relentlessly jumping from one conclusion to the next, laying before you all the terrible things that are going to happen if you do not pass that exam. You start being consumed by stress and anxiety, and your mind starts losing its ability to think clearly. When this happens, force yourself to take a step back and do the following:

- Step 1: Ask yourself what the worst-case scenario is. The worst-case scenario here would be for you to fail the exam and get denied admission to your favorite university.

- Step 2: Take some time to mentally accept the worst-case scenario should it materialize, i.e., not being admitted into your favorite university. Then ask yourself, "Is this the end of the world for me? Is my success or failure as a human being truly determined by this one exam? Is my entire future dependent on just this one exam?" Certainly not. For instance, you may still get admitted into other universities even though they are not your number-one choice. Hopefully, you will soon come to the realization that things are not as bad as they first seemed when your mind was clouded by stress and anxiety.

- Step 3: Now that your mind has started to cool down, find ways to mitigate the negative consequences of the worst-case scenario (should it actually materialize in the first place). For instance:

  o You may get accepted to another university and end up being happy there.

  o You may start off your first year in another university, study hard, and then succeed in transferring back to your preferred university.

  o You may successfully complete your bachelor's degree in another university and then transfer back to your preferred university for a master's degree.

The conclusion of this example resembles closely what I personally went through in the past. I was refused admission into my preferred university, which was considered the best in my country. For a while, I felt debilitated, quite upset, and I couldn't think straight. Luckily, I got accepted into another good university, although considered a distant second-best. I went there, completed my bachelor's degree with honors, and then, to my astonishment, received a phone call from my preferred university, offering me a place in one of their renowned master's programs. Apparently, a headhunter in one of their important faculties noticed my impressive grades and decided to give me a call!

Whenever you are facing a situation that seems terrible at first sight, take a step back and analyze it using the above three-step approach. Once your mind is at peace with the worst-case scenario, it will start to relax and function normally again. When that happens, you will naturally realize that things are not as bad as you initially thought and that there are always acceptable solutions, even to the most complicated problems that seemed unsolvable due to stress and anxiety.

SKILL #2

- Ask yourself what the worst-case scenario is.
- Mentally accept it should it materialize.
- Find ways to mitigate its negative consequences.

> "Whenever you're making an important decision, first ask if it gets you closer to your goals or farther away. If the answer is closer, pull the trigger. If it's farther away, make a different choice. Conscious choice making is a critical step in making your dreams a reality."
> —Jillian Michaels

SKILL #3

How to Make an Important Decision

Have you ever felt stressed and anxious when you had to make an important or difficult decision? Have you ever procrastinated making such a decision? The main cause for this is usually a lack of an organized method for making a sound decision. Attempting to soundly solve a problem without a systematic approach will almost always result in failure or a suboptimal solution, which, in turn, leads to additional stress and anxiety.

The next time you are faced with an important decision to make, and you start feeling stressed and anxious about it, stop for a minute, and force yourself to go through the following easy-to-implement, problem-solving approach. With enough practice, this line of action will become second nature to you:

- Step 1: Formulate what the problem is.
- Step 2: Generate alternative solutions.
- Step 3: Evaluate and choose the best solution.
- Step 4: Implement the chosen solution without hesitation.

Step 1: Formulate What the Problem Is

Charles Kettering, the famous inventor and head of research for General Motors, used to say, "A problem well-stated is half-solved." But what is more important for the purpose of this book is that "a problem half-solved" also means diffusing half the stress that is initially associated with it.

In order to accurately state the problem, start by gathering all the relevant factual information that will enable you to make such an informed statement. When going about your fact-gathering mission, be sure to do the following:

- Set aside your emotions and focus only on facts.
- Differentiate facts from opinions.
- Consider all the facts and not just the ones that you feel comfortable with.
- Set a time limit for your fact-gathering mission.

Once all the facts are laid bare before your eyes, formulate in very specific words what the problem is and write it down. Be sure to focus on the root cause of the problem and not on its symptoms. Once you accurately formulate what the problem is, at least half of your stress will dissipate. This, in turn, will free considerable mental resources, allowing you to confidently proceed to step #2.

Step 2: Generate Alternative Solutions

Don't cut corners by thinking you are ready to make a decision just because you know what the problem is. Be patient and persevere throughout this problem-solving approach until the last step. Spending some time to consider the various alternative solutions will add much value to your decision-making process and will open your eyes to new possibilities that you did not consider before. Also, take the time to write down, even if just in a few words, each possible solution that comes to your mind. Writing each of the alternative solutions will help you better formulate them and will facilitate their analysis in step #3.

Step 3: Evaluate and Choose the Best Solution

Objectively analyze and evaluate, without any bias and all emotions set aside, every alternative solution by noting its strengths and weaknesses to tackle the root cause of the problem. To help you objectively determine the weaknesses of each possible solution, start by writing down the strengths of each alternative solution and then play the devil's advocate, opposing whatever strengths you noted. As you diligently go through this process, one solution will start to stand out as better than the rest.

One caveat that you should watch out for at this stage is analysis-paralysis. Analysis-paralysis simply means overanalyzing a given solution to the point where you are unable to pick the optimal one. There is a line beyond which any further analysis is self-destructive and will only lead to additional stress and anxiety. So, be reasonable in your analysis and draw a line beyond which you should stop, decide on the best solution, and move forward to step #4.

Step 4: Implement the Chosen Solution Without Hesitation

Once your decision is taken, implement it without hesitation. Don't stop along the way to doubt yourself or your decision-making process. Having reached this stage, you already know that you did your homework to the best of your abilities and that you could not have done anything better under the circumstances. Have faith and move forward. Once you steadfastly start implementing your decision, the remaining half of your stress will start to dissipate and be replaced with feelings of reassurance and relief.

Let me illustrate the above with a simple example. Suppose that you are the sales manager of a small software company, and an important customer calls you and angrily complains about the latest pricing of one of your software packages. You start feeling stressed and anxious; the last thing you want is to lose an important customer to one of your competitors. Your mind starts jumping left and right, imagining all the possible awful things that are going to happen to you and your company because of this unfortunate situation. Clearly, you won't get anywhere with this mindset. However, being fortunate enough to have read this book, you remember the four-step problem-solving technique, and you decide to give it a try.

Step 1: Formulate What the Problem Is

Start by objectively gathering all the necessary facts surrounding this case. After proper investigation, it turns out that your customer initially misunderstood your company's monthly sales pricing policy, thinking that the discounted software subscription price for the first month would remain the same throughout the first year. Now that you have the necessary facts to proceed with the resolution of this case, formulate in writing exactly what the problem is. It may look like this:

- Customer X misunderstood our software's monthly sales pricing policy, thinking that the discounted software subscription price for the first month would remain the same throughout the first year.

Step 2: Generate Alternative Solutions

Write down the different possible solutions to this problem. For example, you may write this:

- You could call the customer and try to clear up the misunderstanding by re-explaining your company's software monthly subscription pricing policy, namely that the first month's subscription price is only an enticement offer and does not apply to the remainder of the year.

- You could compromise by offering the customer additional separate software to subscribe to at a bundled, discounted subscription price.

- You could persuade your customer to subscribe to a yearly software subscription package instead of the monthly one that he/she currently has and thus offer him/her a better yearly subscription price.

Step 3: Evaluate and Choose the Best Solution

Now that all the possible solutions are laid before your eyes, calmly start analyzing the strengths and weaknesses of each one to decide which one best serves your goals and objectives:

- Chances are that calling the customer to clear up the misunderstanding won't lead anywhere since the customer is very angry and seems to be unwilling to pay the higher monthly subscription price for the remainder of the year.

- Compromising by offering the customer an additional separate software to subscribe to at a bundled, discounted price could work but only if the customer is in need of a new software, which is not certain.

- Gently offering the customer a long-term subscription package at a better price could work if the customer is satisfied with the software. This seems to be the case since no prior complaints were reported by the client about the functionality of the software. Moreover, this solution would actually benefit the company by committing the customer to a one-year contract instead of a monthly one, thus setting the stage for a long-term, successful business relationship.

After careful evaluation, you decide to proceed with the third option and hope for the best.

Step 4: Implement the Chosen Solution Without Hesitation

Now that you have decided on your best course of action, all that remains is to confidently implement it without any hesitation. By now, your initial stress has dissipated, and a clear path to follow is laying within your reach.

SKILL #3
• Formulate the problem. • Generate alternative solutions. • Evaluate and choose the best solution. • Implement without hesitation.

> "There cannot be a stressful crisis next week. My schedule is already full."
> —Henry Kissinger

SKILL #4

Occupy Yourself Constantly

To understand the logic and power behind this particular skill, comfortably lie down on your bed and try to think about two different things at the same time. For instance, try to think about the conversation that you had in the morning with a work colleague and about a movie that you watched a couple of days ago. You will soon realize that you can only think about one or the other at a given point in time but not about both at the same time. And this is because the human brain cannot process two different ideas or thoughts at the same time. The same goes for opposing and conflicting feelings and emotions. For instance, it is practically impossible for you to feel happy and sad, relaxed and tense, or bored and excited at the same time. This just cannot happen. So how can this fact be of any benefit to you in your fight against stress?

Whenever you are feeling stressed, fully occupy yourself with a mentally engaging and absorbing activity. By entirely dedicating yourself to a particular task, your brain will gradually mobilize all its mental resources to that task, up to the point where no available resources are left to entertain feelings of stress. Any task will do as long as it is engaging and requires complete focus and concentration.

If you would like to take this anti-stress technique to the next level, make sure that you occupy yourself constantly all day long. Constantly occupying yourself allows you to slam the door in the face of stress well *before* it has had a chance to infiltrate your mind. From personal experience, I can assure you that you are most vulnerable during those parts of the day when you have enough time on your hands and thus the luxury to start wondering:

- if life in general has any purpose,

- if your life is meaningless,

- if you are turning in circles and getting nowhere, and

- if you have achieved in life whatever you had planned for it.

The list goes on and is, unfortunately, as endless as you can imagine it to be. One way to assist you in plugging all the empty holes in your daily schedule is to apply skill #1 of this book: *compartmentalize your life*. By compartmentalizing your day, you can ensure that it is packed with meaningful and constructive activities that are meant to get you closer to your personal and professional goals. Once you embark on this compartmentalization journey, your enthusiasm and dynamism will hit new levels as you start seeing your goals slowly materialize. Not only will you not have the time or the luxury to feel stressed, but you will also be overcome by feelings of happiness, serenity, and self-fulfillment. These positive feelings are self-feeding and will devour any remaining feelings of stress that you may still be experiencing.

This simple anti-stress technique was echoed by Mr. Lee Iacocca, a renowned American automobile executive best known for the development of the Ford Mustang, Continental Mark III, and Ford Pinto cars while working at the Ford Motor Company in the 1960s and for reviving the Chrysler Corporation as its Chief Executive Officer during the 1980s. He said: "In times of great stress or adversity, it's always best to keep busy, to plow your anger and your energy into something positive."

SKILL #4
Occupy yourself constantly.

> "It isn't the mountain ahead that wears
> you out; it's the grain of sand
> in your shoe."
> —Robert W. Service

SKILL #5:

Don't Mind the Futilities

A long time ago, my father-in-law once told me, "Don't take a firm stance vis-à-vis a secondary issue." Since then, I have never forgotten this wise saying, and I continue to implement its logic to this very day. So, what does it mean? In simple words, don't waste your precious energy and life force on life's endless futilities. Save your fights for the things that really matter the most. Let me illustrate the above with an example from a famous Chinese water torture method.

Chinese water torture consists of holding the body of a person in a still position and subjecting it to slow but continuous drops of water. As long as these drops of water keep falling on the same exact place of the body for a prolonged period of time, each new drop of water eventually starts to carry with it an excruciating amount of pain. Can you imagine a small drop of water causing such unbearable pain? Quite unthinkable, isn't it?

Life's futilities resemble to a large extent these small drops of water. If you allow them to constantly preoccupy you, they will slowly but surely bring havoc. Do not allow yourself to be distracted by pointless and unimportant events, and confidently move past them. One way to do this is by interpreting and dealing with these futilities in a more positive light. The following very simple yet practical example will help illustrate this point.

Suppose that you hate washing the dishes after a long day at work (just like me). Every time it is your turn to wash the dishes after dinner, you struggle hard to get yourself to start with the first dish. Throughout the process, you feel stressed, annoyed, and keep thinking to yourself what a waste of time it is to do this mindless, boring task. Now, in the grand scheme of things, washing the dishes can be considered a futile task. But since there is no escaping from this chore, why not make the most out of it? How so? By merely changing the way you interpret this event, you can drastically alter the way it impacts you.

For instance, washing the dishes can prove to be quite a relaxing activity. The sound of water running and the feeling of soapy bubbles on your skin can be quite a soothing experience, especially if coupled with some background music. Since cleaning the dishes is not a mentally absorbing task, you can make good use of the tranquil time to go through your plans for the next day. By turning this annoying experience into a more pleasant one, you will save yourself some energy and life force for the more serious and challenging events that surely await you in your life.

I will conclude this chapter with the following quote from Og Mandino, an American author whose books have sold over 50 million copies and have been translated into over twenty-five languages: "Never again clutter your days or nights with so many menial and unimportant things that you have no time to accept a real challenge when it comes along."

SKILL #5
Don't mind futitities.

> "Don't believe every worried thought you have.
> Worried thoughts are notoriously inaccurate."
> —Renee Jain

SKILL #6:

Use Probabilities to Control Your Stress

I would like to start off this chapter by providing you with three interesting pieces of statistics:

- According to the US's Centers for Disease Control and Prevention, about 40 million lightning strikes reach the ground every year throughout the USA. But the chances of an individual being struck by lightning in any given year are less than one in a million (Centers for Disease Control and Prevention, 2022).

- According to the US National Safety Council, flying on a commercial airliner is the safest mode of transport, where the chances of dying as a plane passenger is about 1 in 205,552 versus 1 in 102 for a car crash (SBS News, 2018).

- In the US, considering only the people who go to beaches, an individual's chance of getting attacked by a shark is 1 in 11.5 million, and an individual's chance of getting killed by a shark is less than 1 in 264.1 million (Wikipedia, 2022).

So why am I telling you all this? Because fear and anxiousness do not recognize statistics and probabilities. Fear and anxiousness only show you the ultimate terrifying events without mentioning the probabilities (likelihoods) of these events actually occurring. The next time you feel stressed and anxious about a particular event, take a few minutes to determine the probability of that event actually materializing. Only then will you have a more complete picture of what you are facing. Let me illustrate this with two real-life examples.

Example 1: Fear of Flying

One of my close friends has a terrible fear of flying. He only flies when there are no other available means of transportation. But as soon as he steps onto the plane, he gets overwhelmed by stress and anxiety, he starts sweating, and his heartbeats become harder and faster. In a nutshell, he experiences many of the physiological symptoms of stress that are referred to in the introductory chapter of this book. These symptoms represent the natural response of my friend's body in its attempt to cope with *his perception* that flying is life-threatening and that *he has very little control over it*. But the truth remains that up until this day, my friend has travelled many times and still has not experienced one flight with technical difficulties.

If my friend had taken a few minutes to research that his chances of dying from a plane crash are 1 in 205,552, how much stress and anxiety do you believe he could have spared himself over the years? According to the above undeniable statistics, my friend should fear getting into a car (which he has no problem doing) rather than getting into a plane! Statistics and probabilities don't lie, but misconceived and unfounded stress and anxiety do.

Example 2: Fear of Punks

When I was a young child, I went through a horrible experience that lasted about a month. One of my friends at school told me a terrifying story about a gang of punks about to invade the city where I lived and kidnap young children my age. To my detriment, I believed him. For the next month or so, I dreaded going to sleep. And when I did manage to go to bed, I tried very hard to keep my eyes open for as long as I could, in fear of getting kidnapped as soon as I closed them. I still remember the stress, fear, and agony that I felt every single night. The whole experience was so terrifying that I still vividly remember it as if it were yesterday.

The point here is that the punks never came, and I was never kidnapped. Of course, at the time, I was only a child who got carried away by his friend's wild imagination. But the gist of the story remains the same. In total honesty, what was the probability of punks invading a city and kidnapping young children? Surely, I had a higher chance of being struck by lightning than by being kidnapped in such a way. Had my feeble mind gripped this simple truth, I would have spared myself so many useless, sleepless nights!

So, the next time you are about to feel stressed about a particular event, stop for a minute and determine, in total honesty and without bias, the probability of that event occurring (based on official statistics, your past experience, etc.). By merely going through this mental exercise, your mind will calm down, and a good chunk of your stress and tension will disappear. From thereon, you will be in a much better position to deal with the situation in a more rational, calm, and focused way.

SKILL #6

Use probabilities to control your stress.

> "To accept the inevitable; neither to struggle against it nor murmur at it—this is the greatest lesson of life."
> —Dinah Maria Murlock Craik

SKILL #7:

Accept What You Cannot Avoid or Change

The ability to compartmentalize your life is the most important skill to master to gain better control of your life. Accepting what you cannot avoid or change is perhaps the second most important one. But what do I mean by that? As you may realize by now, there are certain events that you simply cannot avoid or change no matter what you do or how good of a fight you put up. Recognizing these events and accepting them is the best course of action and will spare you enormous amounts of stress. I would like to illustrate this point with the following real-life story.

My father became ill with Parkinson's disease when he was about seventy-four years of age. A few years later, the Parkinson's disease gave way to Alzheimer's. My father eventually died when he was eighty-three years old. During those years, I was living in another country and did not get to see my father much. Moreover, my parents, for some reason, kept my father's illness hidden from me until the symptoms became extremely visible. By the time I knew that my father was very sick, his limbs had already stiffened, and his mental abilities had noticeably declined.

I was heartbroken and in despair. I kept asking my mother whether there was anything more that could be done to help him, whether she had visited all the right doctors, if she gave him all the right medicines, if it were better to keep him in a specialized hospital, etc. My father's sickness tormented me day and night. First, I refused to believe that the twenty-first-century medical community was unable to cure my father's disease. How could science not be able to cure such a disease when it allowed man to harness the power of nuclear energy and send expeditions to the moon? Second, feelings of guilt started running me over. I started wondering whether my troubled childhood relationship with my father had anything to do with the development of this terrible disease and if I should have spent more time with him throughout the years.

Things went on like this for about a year, until I finally resigned and accepted the inevitable: my father's illness had no cure, there was nothing that anyone could have done to avoid it, it was nobody's fault, and I was bound to see his fragile body quickly degrade before my eyes until death do us part. When I came to this stark realization, I felt a deep inner feeling of peace that I had not felt before.

The point of this story is this: do what you can to avoid or change a harmful or unfavorable event. But as soon as you realize that there is no escaping it, stop fighting, and accept it the way it is. By accepting the event as is, you will release all the mental resources that are caught up in fighting a losing battle and smartly reallocate them toward dealing and coping.

While writing this section, certain scenes from my favorite movie, *The Shawshank Redemption*, popped in my head. I visualized what mental shape the prisoners arriving at the Shawshank prison were in. Most of them were apprehensive and in denial vis-à-vis their loss of freedom for years to come. But as time passed, the brightest ones resigned themselves to their new reality, accepted it, and tried to make the best of it. There was no other way for them to survive being incarcerated in such a brutal place. Any other course of action would have led to misery and perhaps insanity. By accepting what cannot be avoided or changed, these prisoners adapted to their new home by focusing all their mental capacity on how to best survive instead of wasting it trying to win a losing battle. I know that this is only a movie, but this is exactly what I would do if, God forbid, I end up in prison one day.

As a conclusion to this chapter, I would like to highlight a famous prayer written by Reinhold Niebuhr, an American theologian, philosopher, commentator on politics and public affairs, and professor at Union Theological Seminary for more than thirty years: "God, grant me the serenity to accept the things I cannot change, courage to change the things I can, and wisdom to know the difference."

SKILL #7
Accept what you cannot avoid or change.

> "There is a tonic strength, in the hour of sorrow
> and affliction, in escaping from the world
> and society and getting back to the simple duties
> and interests we have slighted and forgotten.
> Our simple things have a new charm for us, and we
> suddenly realize that we have been renouncing all
> that is greatest and best, in our pursuit
> of some phantom."
> —William George Jordan

SKILL #8:

Count Your Blessings

Please allow me to ask you an important question: how much is your lung, kidney, heart, pancreas, eye, leg, or arm worth to you? How much would you ask in return for giving away one of your children? I would not give up any of these for all the riches in the world. The point is that all of us have so much more to be thankful for than we care to admit. At times, it can be very easy to lose sight of the many good things that we already have, and this by itself opens the door to vicious feelings of anger, envy, and despair.

"The more grateful I am, the more beauty I see" is a famous quote by Mary Davis, an Irish social entrepreneur, activist, and long-term campaigner for the rights of children and adults with intellectual disabilities. There is a lot of beauty around you. And the more time you take to notice the positives in your life, being grateful for them, the more beauty you will end up seeing.

Make it a habit to count your blessings daily. One smart way to go about this is to keep some sort of a gratitude journal. A gratitude journal is a diary dedicated to reminding you of all the things you are grateful for in life. It may be difficult to start such a diary, but it is certainly worth your time. Write down every positive element in your life no matter how small. You will be surprised how many pages you will fill. Take a couple of minutes each day to supplement it with all the positive elements that keep crossing your life's path. The mere fact of writing and reading this journal will fill your spirit with happiness and serenity. And if you remember *skill 5, occupy yourself constantly*, it is impossible for you to experience opposing and conflicting emotions at the same time. Happiness is bound to kick the sadness out.

I realized how lucky I was in my childhood; I was shocked to learn that my grandfather's right eye was made of glass. Upon my inquiry, my grandfather told me that he lost his eye in a hunting accident when his shotgun malfunctioned and backfired. I spent a couple days trying to find out how living with just one eye would feel by forcing myself to keep my right eye constantly closed. As expected, it turned out to be an extremely unpleasant and difficult experience. When I later asked my grandfather how he was able to bear living with only one eye, he simply told me that he had no other choice but to cope with it (he had to accept what could not be changed). Because of that conversation, I am always thankful for the things I have: my health, family, friends, small house, middle-class job, old, used car, and much more.

If you feel that you don't have enough in life and that you need more to be happy and satisfied, then you must be entirely correct.

Who am I to prove you wrong? But I assure you that you will continue feeling this way for as long as you believe it is true. This vicious circle won't come to an end until you start appreciating the countless blessings that you already have and how lucky you are to have them.

Epictetus, a Greek man who taught philosophy as a way of life rather than merely as a theoretical discipline, said, "He is a wise man who does not grieve for the things which he has not but rejoices for those which he has." Cynthia Ozick, an American short story writer, novelist, and essayist, shared, "We often take for granted the very things that most deserve our gratitude."

SKILL #8

Count Your Blessings.

> "A man is but the product of his thoughts.
> What he thinks, he becomes."
> —Mahatma Gandhi

SKILL #9:

Keep a Positive Mental Attitude

Gautama Buddha said, "We are what we think. All that we are arises with our thoughts. With our thoughts, we make the world." If you think you are happy, you will feel happiness. If you think you are sad, you will feel sadness. If you think you are afraid, you will feel fear. If you think you are tired, you will feel weary. If you think you are excited, you will feel enthusiastic. In a nutshell, you already are what your thoughts are making you to be.

If you are a true believer in the power of your own thoughts, then you already know how important it is to maintain a positive mental attitude. A positive mental attitude is a mindset based on the premise that viewing the upside potential in every situation will attract self-achievement, happiness, and joy. This concept was first introduced back in 1937 by the American self-help author, Napoleon Hill, in his book *Think and Grow Rich*. Key ingredients for this formula are constant doses of hope, courage, and optimism.

People who entertain a positive mental attitude recognize that their reaction to an event is more important than the event itself and that by merely changing the way they interpret an event, they can drastically alter the way it impacts them. Hence, a positive mental attitude affords those who harness it the power to react positively to the events that surround them irrespective of whether these events carry with them a positive or negative outcome.

Individuals who entertain a positive mental attitude start with inner thoughts and feelings of hope, courage, and optimism. Then they project their inner world onto the outside reality. So they end up seeing in their outside reality all the beliefs, emotions, and thoughts of their inner world.

Here are a few ways to help you start building a positive mental attitude. They require perseverance and, most importantly, a lot of practice.

- Focus on the positive things in every situation.

    No matter how challenging or difficult it may seem, try to see a rainbow past a heavy thunderstorm.

- Count your blessings.

    This will increase your optimism and happiness. Stop envying the things you don't have and start appreciating all the things you already have. Keep a gratitude journal to remind you of all the things you are grateful for in life.

- Open up to humor.

    Smiling and laughing have several health benefits, including improved mood, increased positivity, stronger immune system, and decreased stress levels. Laughter triggers the release of three different hormones in your body: dopamine, endorphins, and serotonin, which all contribute to your happiness. This feeling of happiness lowers your stress, anxiety, depression, and physical tension and contributes to better cardiovascular health.

- Surround yourself with positive people.

    Positivity is contagious. Unfortunately, so is negativity. Spend more time with people who think positively, speak positively, act positively, and support your goals and objectives. These people will lift you up and help you focus on the positive things in life. Seek them out and hold on to them like bankers hold on to Swiss gold.

- Practice positive self-talk.

    Self-talk is your internal dialogue (i.e., the voice in your head). Positive self-talk can improve your immune system, physical well-being, and life satisfaction and lower your stress, anxiety, and distress. Whether you blame yourself for everything, focus only on the negative aspects of a situation, or always expect the worst, turn this type of negative thinking into a positive one. For instance, replace "I am weak" with "I am strong," "This won't work" with "Where there is a will, there is a way," "I failed" with "At least I tried," and "It won't work" with "Why not give it a shot and see what happens?" Always be mindful of any negative self-talk that may be going on in your head and immediately replace it with positive self-talk.

- Start your day early on a positive note.

    Wake up early and start your day on a positive note. Take a few minutes to plan your most important tasks for the day, and make sure to fill your head with positive and affirmative statements such as "Today is going to be a wonderful day," "I am going to do my best to get one step closer to my goals and objectives," "I am going to live this day energetically, eagerly, and enthusiastically," "I look forward to living this beautiful day to the fullest," etc.

At times, you may be feeling down, sad, or unenergetic. When this happens, you may find it difficult to change your mood by simply "thinking" it, although it is feasible. Work your way backward by moving to action and commanding your body to act happy and energetic. Force yourself to listen to music or jokes, dance around a bit, sing your favorite song, call up a friend, engage in a fruitful conversation, go out and watch a movie, exercise, etc. Quickly enough, the movements, gestures, and actions of your body will start to positively affect your feelings, emotions, and mood. How can you be feeling down and sad while your actions, gestures, and behavior suggest the opposite?

SKILL #9

Keep a Positive mental attitude.

> "Our greatest weakness lies in giving up.
> The most certain way to succeed
> is always to try just one more time."
> —Thomas Edison

SKILL #10

Never Quit

Are you the kind of person who quits at the first adversity? Do you constantly complain that life never treated you fairly or never gave you an opportunity to achieve and flourish? Do you believe that whatever disadvantages you may have, whether physical, social, or financial, are responsible for your failure? Have you ever heard of Helen Keller, Nick Vujicic, or Esther Vergeer? How about Stephen Hawking, Franklin D. Roosevelt, John Nash, or Andrea Bocelli? Bear with my while I highlight these notable people.

HELEN KELLER

Nature of Disability: Deaf and blind.

Achievements: Hellen Keller became deaf and blind at nineteen months old due to an unknown illness. She got admitted to Radcliffe College in 1900 and graduated with honors in 1904, becoming the first graduate with deaf-blindness in the world. She went on to become a world-class speaker and author. She traveled around the world and campaigned for people with disabilities, women's suffrage, labor rights, and other causes.

NICK VUJICIC

Nature of Disability: Tetra-amelia syndrome (doesn't have arms and legs).

Achievements: Nick Vujicic was born without arms and legs. Despite his struggle with his disability, Nick graduated from Griffith University at the age of twenty-one. He is a world-class motivational speaker and the founder of "Attitude is Altitude." Vujicic's first book, *Life Without Limits: Inspiration for a Ridiculously Good Life*, was published in 2010 and has been translated into more than thirty-two languages.

ESTHER VERGEER

Nature of Disability: Paralysis in legs.

Achievements: Esther was born in 1981 in the Netherlands. Due to an illness that started in 1987, she became paralyzed in March 1990. During her rehabilitation, she learned wheelchair tennis and went professional in 1995. During her career, she won forty-eight Grand Slam tournaments, twenty-three year-end championships, and seven Paralympics titles. Vergeer won the world's No. 1 position in wheelchair tennis in April 1999, regained it in October 2000, and held it up until she relinquished it in January 2013 shortly before her retirement.

STEPHEN HAWKING

Nature of Disability: Amyotrophic lateral sclerosis (ALS).

Achievements: In 1963, at the age of twenty-one, Stephen was diagnosed with early-onset, slow-progressing Amyotrophic lateral sclerosis that gradually paralyzed him. When Stephen lost his speech to ALS in 1985, he began communicating through a speech-generating device. Professor Hawking was one of the most eminent theoretical physicists of his time and made significant contributions in the studies of the origins of the universe, time, big bang theory, black hole radiation, and more.

FRANKLIN D. ROOSEVELT

Nature of Disability: Polio.

Achievements: Franklin D. Roosevelt served as the thirty-second president of the United States from 1933 until his death in 1945. He successfully led the nation through two of its most difficult times: the Great Depression (between 1929 and 1939) and World War II (between 1939 to 1945).

JOHN NASH

Nature of Disability: Acute Paranoid Schizophrenia.

Achievements: John Nash was born in 1928. He began teaching at the Massachusetts Institute of Technology in Princeton University in 1951. In 1959, he was diagnosed with acute paranoid schizophrenia. Despite his continuous struggle with his illness, Nash excelled in the field of mathematics. In 1994, he won the Nobel Prize in Economics for his pioneering analysis of equilibrium in the theory of non-cooperative games (more specifically known as Nash Equilibrium).

ANDREA BOCELLI

Nature of Disability: Completely Blind.

Achievements: Andrea was born in 1958 in Italy and was diagnosed with congenital glaucoma at five months old. He became completely blind when he was twelve years old. Bocelli became a world-famous tenor and songwriter and played the piano, flute, and fiddle.

I am a firm believer that most, if not all, great men and women who left an impressive mark on the world started their journey with a certain adversity, be it physical, social, or financial. Somehow, they were able to find within themselves the necessary courage and discipline to go past their hardships to become great at whatever they chose to pursue. Had they stopped short to lament the situation they were in, they never would have discovered the wonderful possibilities that laid within their reach. But just as importantly, humankind would have lost shining examples to look up to in times of despair and anguish.

The real challenge in life—and perhaps its very essence—is to take misfortune and turn it into a victory. That is something to be venerated and admired for generations to come! And this is exactly why the above individuals, and countless others like them, will always serve as a beacon of hope for humanity.

Now it is your turn. Set aside your fears, weaknesses, and whatever else is holding you back and proceed on the wonderful journey of discovering your possibilities in life. Whatever disadvantages you believe you have, they cannot be harder or tougher than the ones enumerated above. Now, you may not become a world-class speaker or win the Nobel Prize. But the important point here is that you owe it to yourself and your loved ones to overcome whatever hardships you have and make the best of whatever you are already blessed with. So set aside all your excuses and justifications and be on your way.

Along your journey, learn from your mistakes and never quit. Take a couple minutes at the end of each day to ask yourself what you could have done better or differently and apply your conclusions to the next day. Putting your analysis in writing saves it for future reference. Make it a point to move one step closer to your goals with each passing day. By never quitting, you are effectively forcing yourself to think positively, act with courage, and live largely. Irrespective of whether you eventually reach your goals or not, that sort of living is a great triumph and makes your journey throughout life even more worthwhile! This is exactly what the famous expression "The journey is more important than the destination" means.

SKILL #10
Never quit.

> "Don't mind criticism. If it is untrue,
> disregard it; if unfair, keep from irritation;
> if it is ignorant, smile; if it is justified,
> it is not criticism, learn from it."
> —Anonymous

SKILL #11

How to Deal With Criticism

Throughout your journey in life, you will come across many people. Some of them will criticize you and others will hail you. So, how do you deal with them? The last paragraph of *skill 10: never quit* emphasizes the importance of surpassing yourself every single day to help you think positively, act with courage, and live largely. But in order to surpass yourself with each passing day, constructive criticism from your surroundings is necessary. Unfortunately, not all criticism is constructive, and it is important to distinguish between those that are ill-intentioned or ill-founded and those that are worthy of your time and consideration.

The next time you receive criticism, hold your horses and do not get on the defensive too soon. By human nature, most people have trouble accepting negative feedback. However, you should always value anything and everything that will get you closer to your goals, even if it means a bruise to your ego now and then. Start by honestly listening to the critic, and then decide whether the criticism is constructive or not. Constructive criticism looks like this:

- Caring—criticism comes from people who care about you and whom you respect and appreciate.

- Specific—criticism tackles specific elements of your performance and suggests ways for improvement.

- Properly conveyed—criticism resonates with your character and personality for maximum impact and acceptability from your side.

Once you know you are dealing with constructive criticism, immediately capitalize on it by passing to action. Constructive criticism is a rare and valuable opportunity to improve upon yourself, and it should not be wasted through inaction. Also be sure to express your gratitude to the person criticizing you and encourage them to provide you with more of the same.

As for the ill-intentioned or ill-founded criticism, throw them in the garbage bin without any hesitation or second thought, and stay clear of the people who gave them to you. There are many reasons why people may want to harmfully criticize you. Some may be jealous of you. Others simply build their self-esteem and derive great satisfaction by criticizing others. In all cases, you should not care, and certainly you must not give in to your anger in such situations. Just say thank you and be on your way.

The same logic applies to those who hail you. Are they doing it out of self-interest or because of a genuine appreciation of your deeds? Ignore the former and capitalize on the latter by asking them what it is they liked and appreciated in your performance. Also ask them how you can do better next time.

At the end of the day, just make sure to do your best and let your actions and deeds speak for themselves.

SKILL #11

Just do your best and let your deeds speak for themselves.

> "Almost everything will work again if you unplug it for a few minutes, including you."
> —Anne Lamott

SKILL #12

Relax

Learning to properly relax will help you much in countering the negative effects of stress. Mental and physical relaxation helps release tension and restore depleted energy levels, leaving you revitalized and rejuvenated. This is where relaxation techniques come into play. They are free, simple to practice, and can take place virtually anywhere.

The following are some of the benefits of relaxation techniques, just to name a few:

- slowing heart rate,

- lowering of the blood pressure,

- improved focus and mood,

- better sleep quality,

- reduced anger, frustration, and stress levels, and reduced muscle tension.

For maximum effect, use relaxation techniques in conjunction with this book's remaining skills, such as compartmentalizing your life, keeping a positive mental attitude, etc.

There are many relaxation techniques out there:

- yoga,
- aromatherapy,
- meditation,
- deep breathing,
- visualization, and massage.

By quickly searching the internet, you can find all the information you need with respect to each of these techniques. The following are the most important things to keep in mind when it comes to relaxation techniques:

- As with any other skill, they require practice and dedication.
- Consistent practice is paramount for long-lasting effects.
- If one technique does not suit you, replace it with another.
- Use them *before* you feel stressed or as soon as you start experiencing your body's physiological reaction to stress.

One of my personal favorite relaxation techniques is the following:

- I start by closing my eyes and imagining myself in a peaceful and beautiful setting.
- I then move on to my breathing. I relax my breathing rhythm by counting to three while breathing in through my nose and counting to five while breathing out through my mouth. I make it a point to breathe with my belly and not with my lungs (known as diaphragmatic

breathing). My belly comes outward as I take air in and inward as I expel air out. While inhaling, I am absorbing the universe's energy and life force that surround me, and while exhaling, I am expelling my inner stress, anxiety, and tension. With every single breath, I am replacing my innermost negative feelings with the universe's energy and power.

- While maintaining a constant breathing rhythm, I then slowly shift my attention to my body. I focus my mind on each part of my body, starting with my facial muscles and moving down, body part by body part, until I reach my toes. I stop at each body part and make sure that it is totally relaxed and deprived of any tension. Once this is the case, I move on to the next body part until my entire body is totally relaxed.

At the end of my relaxation session, my body and mind are so relaxed that I am incapable of entertaining any harmful feelings like stress and anxiety.

SKILL #12
Relax.

> "For every minute spent organizing,
> an hour is earned."
> —Benjamin Franklin

SKILL # 13

Dealing With Stress in the Workplace

All the previously mentioned skills can be easily applied for managing stress in the workplace. But I would like to dedicate this chapter to additional tips that are specifically intended to deal with workplace stress.

Keeping Your Work Desk Organized

Having a cluttered and disorganized desk is extremely unproductive and very stressful to look at. Follow these simple tips for a more productive working environment that will help you stay on top of your work:

- Position your computer screen in front of you so that it is between forty and seventy-five centimeters from your eyes. The top part of the screen should be level with your eyes when you are sitting straight up.

- Keep whatever you often use close to your dominant hand, be it a phone, a stapler, pens, Post-it notes, etc.

- Only keep on your desk what you need to complete your work. If you only need one pen, keep the rest in a drawer. If you have food, keep it in the fridge or in a drawer. If you have a document that you only use once per day or less often, file it away.

- Use Post-it notes to remind you of the urgent tasks you need to attend to but not as a to-do list. To-do lists are better maintained in a digital format, and keeping lists on Post-its will result in countless notes scattered all over your desk and monitor.

- Don't let paper documents pile up on your desk. Attend to them as soon as they reach your desk and immediately file them away.

- Use productivity software to reduce the amount of paper, notifications, and reminders that pass through your desk rather than keeping them on pieces of paper scattered all over your desk and computer monitor. There are many simple and easy-to-use productivity programs to help you track your tasks, appointments, meetings, deadlines, etc.

Managing Emails

Emails have become a necessity in the workplace and having to deal with their large number on a daily basis can quickly overwhelm you and increase your stress levels. Here are a few pointers that will assist you in better managing your daily emails:

- Not all communications are best suited for emails. Some communications are best conveyed through telephone calls, face-to-face or virtual meetings, messaging, etc. Remember that the more emails you send, the more emails you will receive and thus have to manage. So always ask yourself whether an email is the best form of communication for your message.

- Allocate one or more daily time buckets for specifically dealing with emails. For instance, you may decide to exclusively deal with your emails every day between 9:00 A.M. and 10:00 A.M. and between 2:00 P.M. and 3:00 P.M. Restrict the time you spend on your emails to these time buckets only. Make sure to inform your work colleagues accordingly and advise them how to contact you by other means in case an urgent situation comes up in between.

- Group emails into meaningful folders and subfolders for future ease of reference. As soon as you finish dealing with an email, file it under the most relevant folder.

- When you open an email, deal with it instantaneously if you can. Keeping emails in your inbox and revisiting them at a later stage only adds to the amount of time it takes to process them. Make it a point to resolve emails as soon as you can, and then file them accordingly.

- Read email threads in reverse chronological order, that is from the newest email to the oldest one. If you start reading the oldest email first, you may be tempted to enter into the conversation before realizing the problem has already been resolved. Answering emails before reading all material will entail confusion, especially if your instructions or advice is counter to what has already been discussed.

- Ask your work colleagues to ensure that the latest title of an email thread is reflective of its most recent content as many email threads start off with a given title and then move on to a completely unrelated topic but continue to show the same initial (but now misleading) title.

Managing Meetings

There is nothing more time-consuming and stressful than attending unproductive meetings. Stick to the following few pointers for shorter yet more productive meetings:

• Meetings are usually time-consuming and sometimes not required. Just like emails, always question whether a meeting is necessary in the first place or if alternative means of communication are better suited under the circumstances.

• If a meeting is necessary, then it should be coupled with an agenda. The meeting's agenda clearly describes objectives, a list of topics to be discussed, a list of attendees, a start time, a duration, a location, and any documents that the attendees need to familiarize themselves with prior to attending the meeting.

• Only the minimum number of people should be invited to the meeting. The more people there are, the higher the chances of sidetracking from the initial purpose.

• Keep the meetings short, preferably within one hour. Long meetings open the way for boredom, sidetracking, and unproductivity.

• For large meetings, assigning roles is important. Decide beforehand as to whom will take minutes of the meeting, who will remind everyone to remain on topic as soon as the conversations begin to sidetrack, who will alert everyone when it is time to start wrapping up the meeting, etc.

• Ask everyone to turn their phones off and refrain from multitasking (such as responding to emails, having side conversations, etc.).

• Meetings should start on time. Do not wait for latecomers; this will only

result in wasting everyone else's time. By the same token, meetings should end on time unless their objectives are reached in less time.
- Encourage attendees to participate and be creative. Actively participating attendees tend to have more energy, feel more enthusiastic, and certainly much less stress than passive ones.

- Make sure the meeting concludes with a specific action plan that clearly states what needs to be done, by whom, and when. Also, leave room for questions and answers to ensure that everyone is clear on their responsibilities and associated accountabilities.

Role-Playing

At times, some work-related tasks can become extremely stressful, not because of their complexity or associated deadlines but because of their dullness and tediousness. Generally, we are much more excited and energized by challenging tasks that promote self-achievement rather than mundane activities. Unfortunately, we all must deal with the latter occasionally, and role-playing is the best way to deal with them. This concept is best illustrated with the following real-life example.

Back in the days when I was a bank controller, an important part of my job consisted of reviewing the credit worthiness of banks' loan portfolios. This entailed visiting a given bank and reviewing its loans that exceeded a certain threshold. In order to complete my assignment, my team and I sometimes had to review hundreds of credit files, a task that quickly turned tedious at certain times. I found that the best way to go about my job as painlessly as possible was to pretend that I was a government agent visiting a highly secretive corporation to uncover substantial irregularities in its dealings and transactions. This role-playing worked miracles for me and made my job a whole lot easier. By changing the framework and settings, I put more excitement into a task that otherwise would have been extremely dull.

As pointed out earlier, you are what your thoughts make you to be. So, if you think you are excited about what you are doing, you will quickly feel enthusiastic about doing it. And the only person who can add a sense of excitement and challenge to an otherwise boring activity is you.

SKILL #13: DEALING WITH STRESS IN THE WORKPLACE

- Keep your work desk organized.
- better manage your emails and settings
- Deal with tedious taks with role play.

> "If you don't make time for exercise,
> you'll probably have to
> make time for illness."
> —Robin Sharma

SKILL #14

Exercise Consistently

No book that deals with managing stress can claim to be complete without discussing exercising. Physical activity should be an integral part of any arsenal that is dedicated to fighting stress.

I was never really into sports. I practiced karate for about three years when I was fifteen years old to learn to defend myself against a high school bully. But apart from that, I never played any sport in any consistent manner until I reached forty-two years old. At that time, I was suffering from severe lower back pain caused by two degenerative lower back disks. A competent doctor advised me to take my condition seriously and start strengthening my core muscles to better support my trunk and relieve some of the pressure surrounding my disks. Left with no other choice, I forced myself to start exercising in the gym with a special emphasis on my core muscles, and I have never stopped exercising since then. What started out as a requirement for a specific medical condition quickly evolved into a way of life that has helped me deal with stress.

From personal experience, I can assure you that consistent exercising should become one of your main weapons in your fight against stress. Find below a few of the many benefits of consistent exercising, as these specifically relate to managing stress:

- Exercising increases the production of the endorphin neurotransmitters. The endorphin neurotransmitters trigger a positive feeling in the body similar to that of morphine. This is the "happiness" feeling that is also commonly referred to as the "runners' high."

- During a good workout, you will notice that your attention and focus quickly shift from your day's worries and troubles toward your body's movements and gestures. The end result is a good dose of relief and positivity.

- After exercising, your self-confidence is boosted, your stress levels are down, your mood is better, and you feel more relaxed and energized than when you first started your workout.

But in order to have lasting effects, exercising needs to be consistent and an integral part of your lifestyle. Here are a few pointers that will help you remain consistent when it comes to exercising:

- Start by enumerating, in writing, all the benefits that you will derive from regular exercising and come to grips with the fact that exercising is just as important as eating, drinking, sleeping, and working. Your body was not designed to remain idle but rather to move and be active. The label that came with your body that you may have missed reads, "Use me or lose me!"

- Set specific goals that are achievable, measurable, and time specific.

- Your goals must be achievable; otherwise, you will quickly lose interest in pursuing what can never be reached.

- Your goals should be measurable in the sense that you should be able to determine at any time how far and how long you still have to go in order to achieve them.

- Goals with no time limits lack the necessary pressure to keep you committed to exercising in the long run. Without time specificity and the associated pressure, it might take you forever to achieve your goals, a demotivating thought in its own right.

- Break down your larger goals into smaller ones. Large goals are intimidating and will quickly put you off from exercising. Smaller goals are not only more achievable but also faster to reach. Reaching these smaller goals will help sustain your motivation throughout your exercising routine and gradually build up your self-confidence.

- Keep an accurate log to track your progress and remind you to stay on track. As you see yourself slowly move closer to your goals, your sense of achievement will help you remain committed to your exercising schedule.

- If you believe in peer pressure, then why not publicize your goals to your close friends and family and ask them to help you stick with exercising?

- Surround yourself with a few gym-goers. These could be friends, family members, neighbors, or work colleagues. The benefit here is mutual. When one feels the urge to skip exercising, the others will ensure that he/she won't.

- Make exercise a fun activity rather than a chore. The more you enjoy exercising, the higher the chances you will stick to it. Keep note of all the things you enjoy while exercising (music, gym atmosphere, sight of other people exercising, the energy and happiness you feel at the end of your workout, etc.) and repeat them in your mind every time you feel the urge to skip exercising.

- Choose a convenient fitness location to avoid excuses like traffic or long distance.

- Do whatever it takes to fight the initial urge to skip exercising. The hardest part of exercising is usually the first fifteen minutes when all your bodily chemical reactions are set into motion. Once you are beyond that stage, your body and mood will take control and carry you flawlessly to the end of your exercising session.

- Most importantly, do not listen to excuses. These are endless, and they come in all shapes and forms. Here are just a few:

    o It is raining outside, so I better skip training today.

    o I had a terrible day at work, and I just want to sleep.

    o What is the big deal if I skip training today and exercise tomorrow instead?

    o I just don't feel like exercising today.

    o I am under pressure at work, and therefore I do not have the time to exercise today.

The best way to deal with the above excuses is to simply ignore them and recognize that your feelings toward exercising are totally irrelevant. This is so important that I am going to repeat it: your feelings toward exercising are totally irrelevant. Replace all the above self-talk with just this one:

   o I don't need motivation to exercise. Motivation is about

waiting until I feel I want to exercise. I only need discipline. Discipline is about exercising irrespective of how I feel about it because it is something that I know I have to do. So, I better get on with it.

This kind of discipline is reflected in Nike's iconic slogan: "Just do it." This slogan was created back in 1988 by Dan Wieden, the cofounder of the advertising firm Wieden and Kennedy. In an interview with Design Indaba, Wieden revealed that the slogan was inspired by the following final words of a death-row prisoner who was facing execution: "You know, let's do it." After reading it, Dan Wieden was astonished at how this inmate was able to muster the necessary courage to push through his execution and thus decided to build upon the inmate's final words to come up with Nike's legendary slogan.

Incorporate exercising into your lifestyle so it becomes an integral part of your personal journey to a healthier and happier life.

SKILL #14
Exercise consistently.

> "I want you to think of your life as an hourglass. You know there are thousands of grains of sand in the top of the hourglass; and they all pass slowly and evenly through the narrow neck in the middle. Nothing you or I could do would make more than one grain of sand pass through this narrow neck without impairing the hourglass. You and I and everyone else are like this hourglass."
> —Dale Carnegie

CONCLUSION

Your life is like an hourglass. Look at the hourglass very carefully. Each grain of sand represents a day in your life. The upper part of the hourglass represents the days that you still have left on this earth; that is your future. The bottom part represents the days that have gone by; that is your past. The middle part, where each grain of sand moves from the upper part to the lower part, represents your present, i.e., today. There is much to be learned from this simple but genius machine:

- Whatever you do and no matter how hard you try, you can never take one single grain of sand from the bottom part of the hourglass and put it back in the upper part. That is because your past does not exist anymore. *Leave your past where it belongs, in the past, and do not mourn it.*

- Whatever you do and no matter how hard you try, you never get to decide which grain of sand from the top part of the hourglass gets to filter down to the bottom part. That is because your future does not exist yet. *Leave your future where it belongs, in the future, and do not think about it.*

- The most interesting part of the hourglass is its middle part. This is your present, i.e., today. This is the only part of the hourglass where you get to decide on anything. And whatever you do, you can never fit more than one grain of sand in the middle part of the hourglass at the same time. *Live one day at a time, to its fullest, by being here and now.*

Not everyone will wake up in the morning, and not everyone will go to bed at night. If you are amongst the fortunate ones who get to wake up and spend today, live it with all the energy, enthusiasm, and vitality that you can muster and with as little stress as possible. A day well lived constitutes a solid foundation for a better tomorrow and a pleasant dream once it merges with your past.

Before you close this book, take a minute to recall all the skills you learned and commit to practicing them diligently every day. Mastering these skills requires time, effort, perseverance, and lots of practice. But it is certainly worth it. Life is too short to be lived in stress. Unlock your best possibilities by doing away with stress, and become the best possible version of yourself.

I now leave you with a famous quote by Benjamin Disraeli, a British statesman who served twice as prime minister of the United Kingdom: "Life is too short to be little. Man is never so manly as when he feels deeply, acts boldly, and expresses himself with frankness and with fervor."

> "Give your stress wings and let it fly away."
> —Terri Guillemets

www.ingramcontent.com/pod-product-compliance
Lightning Source LLC
LaVergne TN
LVHW041542070526
838199LV00046B/1804